MW01005264

MEXICAN SAYINGS:
THE TREASURE OF A PEOPLE

Dichos Mexicanos:
El Tesoro de un Pueblo

By
Octavio A. Ballesteros, Ed.D.
&
María del Carmen Ballesteros, M.Ed.

EAKIN PRESS　★　Austin, Texas

Published in the United States of America
By Eakin Press
An Imprint of Sunbelt Media, Inc.
P.O. Drawer 90159   ★   Austin, TX 78709-0159

ISBN 0-89015-810-X

Library of Congress Cataloging-in-Publication Data

Mexican sayings : the treasure of a people = Dichos mexicanos : el tesoro de una gente / [compiled] by Octavio A. Ballesteros & María del Carmen Ballesteros.
       p.   cm.
   ISBN 0-89015-810-X : $14.95
   1. Proverbs, Mexican.   I. Ballesteros, Octavio A., 1936–.   II. Ballesteros, María del Carmen.   III. Title: Dichos mexicanos.
PN6495.M4M48   1992
398.9′61′0972--dc20
                                                                91-18953
                                                                CIP

To the late Felix H. Morales. May his countless good deeds long be remembered by the people of Houston, Texas.

CONTENTS

PREFACE

A saying is a concise, popular statement, often moralistic in nature, which expresses what most individuals believe to be true. Sayings are used to illustrate a point, settle an argument, advise an acquaintance, friend or relative, or simply to amuse the listener. There are some learned individuals who insist on making fine distinctions between such things as sayings, proverbs, maxims, adages, aphorisms and axioms. Other individuals cannot agree on whether a saying and a proverb are synonymous terms. Some individuals, of course, maintain that a saying is an utterance that has not yet achieved proverbial status; or to put it another way, that a proverb is a saying that has achieved cultural and linguistic "immortality." In this book, a saying is a proverb and a proverb is a saying, while a maxim is an adage and an adage is an aphorism and possibly an axiom. Though there may exist subtle differences among these terms, let there be no doubt that this is a book of Mexican sayings.

Who can say with certainty that a particular utterance is a saying and that another is not? Well, the compilers of this anthology are of the opinion that an utterance is a saying if they feel that it is one.

A saying, whatever its national origin, tends to have no easily discernible author; anonymity is a common characteristic of sayings of every language and culture. Yet, the origin of many sayings can be traced to a specific personage, writer or literary work.

It can be said that sayings are part of the cultural treasure of a people because the wisdom, wit, philosophy, psychology and social values of a cultural group are preserved in their sayings. Without a doubt, the sayings of a people are a manifestation of their culture's personality, character and spirit.

Actually, Mexican sayings are the treasure of many ages and cultures. For example, though some Mexican sayings originated in Spain, some Spanish sayings are of Moslem origin. As most students of Spanish history know, Moslems were in control of large areas of Spain from 711 A.D. to 1492 A.D. It is not surprising that the Spanish culture and language have been so strongly influenced by the Moslem world. When the Spaniards arrived in Mexico during the early sixteenth century, they brought their sayings with them. Eventually, many of the Spanish sayings used in Mexico by the Spaniards were affected by the cultures and languages of the indigenous Mexicans — the First Mexicans — who also are referred to as Mexican Indians. The observant reader may notice that some Mexican sayings contain concepts which are of Mexican Indian origin. The reader also may notice that some Mexican sayings have a biblical origin, while other Mexican sayings have a philosophical origin.

Those who have studied the ancient sayings of Spain and compared them with the present-day sayings of Mexico probably will conclude that Spanish sayings, though full of truth and sagacity, are somewhat dry and not nearly as vivid and interesting as the sayings of Mexico. Spanish sayings, like Spanish food, tend to pale when compared to Mexican sayings and Mexican food.

A knowledge of Mexican sayings provides an individual with a better understanding of Mexico, the Mexican people, the Mexican American, other Hispanic American cultural groups, and the people of Spanish America.

Mexicans who live on farms and ranches and in small towns tend to use sayings more frequently than Mexicans who live in large cities, and older Mexicans tend to use sayings more frequently than young Mexicans. It is understandable that Mexican Americans would use Mexican sayings less often than the people of Mexico, because many Mexican Americans are in the process of forgetting the little Spanish that they know. The fact that so many Mexican Americans are not familiar with the sayings of Mexico is a strong argument for the publication of a book on Mexican sayings and making it available to Mexican Americans of all ages.

Perhaps American school students who are exposed to the sayings of another culture will become interested in learning the sayings of their own culture. The study of foreign sayings can help students develop an appreciation for cultural and linguistic differences in people. Also, the study of sayings

vi

can help students develop an interest in the past and a respect for our society's elderly.

This collection of sayings was compiled primarily for the person who wants to learn more about the culture and language of Mexico. The compilers hope that this book will contribute to a better understanding of the Mexican mentality, personality, character and manner of behavior. This collection also should prove useful to the person who wishes to compare Mexican sayings with the sayings of another culture and language.

One objective of this collection is to provide the reader with a deeper understanding of and appreciation for the Spanish language as spoken by Mexicans and some Mexican Americans. Another objective of this collection is to produce a book which can be used as a supplementary reader by students in Spanish language courses. The compilers of this work believe that a book of sayings, when properly utilized, can be an effective tool to motivate foreign language learners.

It took the compilers more than four years to collect the sayings contained in this work, which were contributed by dozens of Mexican citizens and Mexican Americans. Each contributor was either a resident of Texas or of northern Mexico.

The more than four hundred Mexican sayings in this compilation were obtained primarily from interviews with elderly Mexican citizens and Mexican Americans. Many sayings were gathered from conversations with friends, relatives, in-laws and acquaintances. Some sayings were obtained from Mexican motion pictures and from radio and television announcers who used Mexican sayings in their conversations. Finally, a few sayings were acquired at parties and other social gatherings through the utilization of the "conversational eavesdropping" technique.

The sayings in this compilation have been classified under seven categories: (1) sayings about love, (2) humorous sayings, (3) philosophical sayings, (4) religious sayings, (5) sayings that advise, (6) psychological sayings, and (7) sayings about animals. Each Mexican saying has been translated into English from Spanish. Most sayings have been translated literally. However, when the literal translation failed to convey the full meaning of the Mexican saying, the saying also was paraphrased. In some instances, English parallels to Mexican sayings are provided.

Those readers who enjoyed reading Octavio A. Ballesteros' *Mexican Proverbs: The Philosophy, Wisdom and Humor of a People* probably will enjoy reading *Mexican Sayings: The Treasure of a People*. Both books contain short, ingenious, popular statements from the Mexican culture and Spanish language that express obvious truths.

Anyone who has ever attempted to write a book can attest to the fact that it is no easy task to complete a literary work, even when two writers are coauthoring the work. The completion of this book was facilitated by the assistance of the following persons: María B. Gonzales, María Elena Palacios, Aurora G. Rodriguez, Glodomiro E. González, Hector E. Rodriguez, Jorge B. González and Emma G. Cavazos.

OCTAVIO A. BALLESTEROS
MARÍA DEL CARMEN BALLESTEROS
San Antonio, Texas

PREFACIO

Un dicho es un relato conciso y popular, frecuentemente moralizador en esencia, que expresa lo que muchos individuos creen sea verdad. Los dichos son usados para ilustrar un punto, aclarar un argumento, aconsejar a un conocido, amigo o pariente, o simplemente para divertir al escuchante. Hay algunos hombres letrados que insisten en hacer distinciones refinadas, entre ciertas cosas como dichos, proverbios, máximas, adagios, aforismos, y axiomas. Otros individuos no pueden ponerse de acuerdo si un dicho y un proverbio son términos sinónimos. Algunos individuos, por supuesto, sostienen que un dicho es una declaración que todavía no ha logrado estado proverbial; o para ponerlo de otra manera, un proverbio es un dicho que ha alcanzado "inmortalidad" cultural y lingüística. En este libro, un dicho es un refrán y un refrán es un dicho, mientras que una máxima es un adagio y un adagio es un aforismo y posiblemente un axioma. Aunque pueden existir unas diferencias sutiles entre estos términos, que no haya ninguna duda que éste es un libro de dichos mexicanos.

¿Quién puede decir con seguridad que una declaración particular es un dicho y que otra no lo es? Los compiladores de esta antología son de la opinión que una declaración es un dicho si ellos sienten que lo es.

Un dicho, sea lo que fuere su origin nacional, tiende no tener un autor fácilmente reconocible; la anonimia es una característica común de dichos de todas las culturas y todos los idiomas. Sin embargo, el origen de muchos dichos puede ser trazado a un personaje específico, a un escritor o a una obra literaria.

Se puede decir que los dichos son parte del tesoro cultural de un pueblo porque la sabiduría, viveza, filosofía, psicología y valores sociales de un grupo cultural son preservados en sus dichos. Sin ninguna duda, los dichos de un pueblo son la manifestación de la personalidad, carácter y espíritu de su cultura.

Efectivamente, los dichos mexicanos son el tesoro de muchas épocas y culturas. Por ejemplo aunque algunos dichos mexicanos originaron en España; algunos dichos españoles son de origen musulmán. Como la mayor parte de los estudiantes de historia española saben, los musulmanes estuvieron en dominio de grandes áreas de España del 711 A.C. al 1492 A.C. No hay que sorprenderse que la cultura y la lengua española hayan sido fuertemente influidas por el mundo musulmán. Por consiguiente, cuando los españoles llegaron a México durante el principio del siglo diez y seis, trajeron sus dichos con ellos. Con el tiempo, muchos de los dichos españoles usados en México por los españoles fueron afectados por las culturas y los idiomas de los mexicanos indigenas — los primeros mexicanos — a los que también se les refiere como indios mexicanos. El lector observante notará que algunos dichos mexicanos contienen conceptos que originaron de los indios mexicanos. El lector también notará que algunos dichos mexicanos tienen un origin bíblico mientras otros dichos mexicanos tienen un origin filosófico.

Los que han estudiado los dichos antiguos de España y los han comparado con los dichos de México de hoy probablemente concluirán que los dichos españoles, aun cuando están llenos de verdad y sagacidad, son algo insípidos y ni siquiera tan animados e interesantes como los dichos de México. Los dichos españoles, como la comida española, tienden a palidecer cuando se comparan con los dichos mexicanos y la comida mexicana.

Un conocimiento de los dichos mexicanos provee a un individuo con un mejor entendimiento de México, la gente de México, el méxicoamericano, otros grupos culturales hispanoamericanos, y la gente de Hispanoamérica.

Los mexicanos que viven en haciendas, ranchos y poblaciones tienden usar dichos más frecuentemente que los mexicanos que viven en ciudades grandes y los ancianos mexicanos tienen la tendencia de usar dichos más frecuentemente que los mexicanos jóvenes. Se comprende que los méxicoamericanos usan los dichos mexicanos menos frecuentemente que la gente de México, porque muchos méxicoamericanos están en el proceso de olvidar el poco español que ellos saben. El hecho de que tantos méxicoamericanos no están familiarizados con los dichos de México es un argumento poderoso para la publicación de un libro sobre dichos mexicanos y hacerlo disponible a méxicoamericanos de todas las edades.

Tal vez los estudiantes de las escuelas norteamericanas que son expuestos a los dichos de otra cultura se interesarán en aprender los dichos de su propia cultura. El estudio de dichos extranjeros puede ayudar estudiantes a desarrollar un aprecio para las diferencias culturales y lingüísticas de la gente. Del mismo modo, el estudio de dichos puede ayudar estudiantes a desarrollar un interés en el pasado y un respeto a los ancianos de nuestra sociedad.

Esta colección de dichos fue compilada principalmente para la persona que desea aprender más tocante a la cultura y el idioma de México. Los compiladores esperan que este libro contribuya a un mejor entendimiento de la mentalidad, personalidad, carácter y comportamiento del mexicano. Asi mismo esta colección deberá probarse provechosa para la persona que desea comparar dichos mexicanos con los dichos de otra cultura y otro idioma.

Un objetivo de esta colección es para proveer al lector con una comprensión y una apreciación más profunda por el idioma español como es hablado por mexicanos y algunos méxicoamericanos. Otro objetivo de esta colección es para producir un libro que se pueda usar como un libro suplementario de lectura para estudiantes del idioma español. Los compiladores de esta obra opinión que un libro de dichos, cuando es utilizado adecuadamente, puede ser un instrumento efectivo para motivar a estudiantes de idiomas extranjeros.

Les tomó más de cuatro años a los compiladores para colectar los dichos contenidos en esta obra, los cuales fueron contribuidos por docenas de ciudadanos mexicanos y méxicoamericanos. Cada contribuyente era un residente de Tejas o del norte de México.

Los más de cuatro cientos dicho mexicanos en esta compilación fueron obtenidos primeramente de entrevistas con ciudadanos mexicanos y méxicoamericanos de edad avanzada. Muchos dichos fueron reunidos de conversaciones con amigos, parientes, parientes políticos y conocidos. Algunos dichos fueron obtenidos de películas mexicanas y de anunciadores de radio y televisión que usan dichos mexicanos en sus conversaciones. Finalmente, algunos dichos fueron adquiridos en fiestas y otras reuniones sociales, donde los compiladores escucharon a los invitados usar dichos.

Los dichos en esta compilación han sido clasificados bajo siete categorias: (1) dichos de amor, (2) dichos humorísticos, (3) dichos filosóficos, (4) dichos religiosos, (5) dichos consejeros, (6) dichos psicológicos, y (7) dichos de animales. Cada dicho mexicano ha sido traducido al inglés del español. La mayor parte han sido traducidos literalmente. No obstante, cuando la tradución literal no logró comunicar el significado completo del dicho mexicano, el dicho también fue parafraseado. En algunos casos, paralelos en inglés a los dichos mexicanos, son proporcionados.

Aquellos lectores que disfrutaron leyendo el libro *Mexican Proverbs: The Philosophy, Wisdom and Humor of a People (Proverbios mexicanos: la filosofía, sabiduría y humor de un pueblo)* de Octavio A. Ballesteros probablemente gozarán leyendo *Mexican Sayings: The Treasure of a People (Dichos mexicanos: el tesoro de un pueblo)*. Ambos libros contienen declaraciones breves, ingenuas y populares de la cultura mexicana y del idioma español que expresan verdades obias.

Cualquiera persona que alguna vez haya intentado escribir un libro puede afirmar al hecho de que no es una tarea fácil completar una obra literaria, aun cuando dos escritores están colaborado en la obra. La realización de este libro fue facilitada por la asistencia de las siguiente personas: María B. Gonzales, María Elena Palacios, Aurora G. Rodriguez, Glodomiro E. González, Hector E. Rodriguez, Jorge B. González y Emma G. Cavazos.

OCTAVIO A. BALLESTEROS
MARÍA DEL CARMEN BALLESTEROS
San Antonio, Texas

SUGGESTED WAYS TO USE THIS BOOK

— Give this book as a gift to a Hispanic friend who enjoys reading books written in the Spanish language.

— High school and college students who are studying Spanish can use the sayings in this book to gain deeper insights into the Hispanic culture.

— The sayings in this collection can be used by persons who want to learn more about Mexico, Mexicans, Mexican Americans and the Spanish language.

— Because *Mexican Sayings* is a Spanish-English bilingual book, this anthology can be used by English speakers who want to learn Spanish and by Spanish speakers who want to learn English. *Mexican Sayings* should prove especially useful to the thousands of persons who recently have immigrated to the United States from Spanish America.

— Persons who have enjoyed reading Octavio A. Ballesteros' *Mexican Proverbs* also will enjoy reading *Mexican Sayings* because both books contain related material.

— An anthology of Mexican sayings is the type of book that tends to put a smile on the reader's face; thus, this is a "happy book" which can be given to anyone who can appreciate the wise, witty and moralistic messages which are found in many of the sayings of Mexico.

MODOS SUGERIDOS PARA EL USO
DE ESTE LIBRO

Regale este libro a un amigo hispano que se divierte leyendo libros escritos en español.

— Estudiantes de la escuela secundaria y de la universidad que están estudiando español pueden usar los dichos de este libro para ganar una comprensión más profunda a la cultura hispana.

— Los dichos en esta colección pueden ser usados por personas que quieren aprender más acerca de México, los mexicanos, los méxicoamericanos y el idioma español.

— Debido a que *Mexican Sayings (Dichos mexicanos)* es un libro bilingüe en español e inglés, esta antología puede ser usada por personas de habla inglés que desean aprender español y por personas de habla española que quieren aprender inglés. *Mexican Sayings (Dichos mexicanos)* deberá probarse particularmente beneficioso a los millares de personas que recientemente han inmigrado de Hispanoamérica a los Estados Unidos.

— Las personas que han disfrutado leyendo el libro *Mexican Proverbs (Proverbios mexicanos)* de Octavio A. Ballesteros también disfrutarán leyendo *Mexican Sayings (Dichos mexicanos)*, porque ambos libros contienen material relacionado.

— Una antología de dichos mexicanos es la clase de libro que tiende poner una sonrisa en el semblante del lector; de esa manera, éste es un "libro alegre" que se puede obsequiar a cualquiera persona que pueda apreciar los mensajes juiciosos, graciosos y moralizadores que se encuentran en muchos de los dichos de México.

REFERENCES

The authors recommend the following references to those readers interested in learning more about Mexico, the Mexican culture, and the Spanish language.

Alba, Victor. *The Mexicans: The Making of a Nation.* New York: Frederick A. Praeger, Publishers, 1967.

Ballesteros, Octavio A. *Mexican Proverbs: The Philosophy, Wisdom and Humor of a People.* Burnet, Texas: Eakin Press, 1979.

Barker, Marie E. *Español Para el Bilingüe.* Skokie, Illinois: National Textbook Company, 1973.

Celorio, Marta, and Annette C. Barlow. *Handbook of Spanish Idioms.* New York: Regents Publishing Company, 1973.

Fisher, Howard T., and Marion Hall Fisher (editors). *Life in Mexico: The Letters of Fanny Calderón de la Barca.* Garden City, New York: Doubleday & Company, Inc., 1966.

Flandrau, Charles M. *Viva Mexico!* Urbana: University of Illinois Press, 1964.

Flores, Angel (editor). *Spanish Stories/Cuentos Españoles: A Bantam Dual Language Book.* New York: Bantam Books, 1971.

Lewis, Oscar. *Life in a Mexican Village: Tepoztlán Restudied.* Urbana: University of Illinois Press, 1963.

Marett, Robert. *Mexico.* New York: Walker and Company, 1971.

Nash, Rose. *Comparing English and Spanish: Patterns in Phonology and Orthography.* New York: Regents Publishing Co., 1977.

Nicholson, Irene. *The X in Mexico.* Garden City, New York: Doubleday & Company, Inc., 1966.

Robe, Stanley Linn. *Mexican Tales and Legends from Los Altos.* Berkeley: University of California Press, 1970.

Stoppelman, Joseph W. F. *People of Mexico.* New York: Hastings House, 1966.

Strand, Mark (editor). *New Poetry of Mexico.* New York: E. P. Dutton & Co., 1970.

Treviño, Elizabeth Barton. *My Heart Lies South: The Story of My Mexican Marriage.* New York: Crowell, 1953.

Varona, Esteban Antonio de. *A Handbook of Mexican Treasures.* Mexico, D. F: Unión Gráfica, S.A., 1958.

Villacano, Eugenio. *Viva Morelia.* New York: M. Evans, 1971.

West, John O. *Mexican-American Folklore.* Little Rock, Arkansas: August House, 1988.

Wilhelm, John. *John Wilhelm's Guide to All Mexico.* New York: McGraw-Hill Book Company, 1973.

MEXICAN SAYINGS:
THE TREASURE OF A PEOPLE

Dichos Mexicanos:
El Tesoro de un Pueblo

DICHOS DE AMOR/SAYINGS ABOUT LOVE

1

Afortunado en el amor, desafortunado en el juego.

a. Fortunate in love, unfortunate in gambling.
b. Lucky in love, unlucky in gambling.

2

Boda retrazada, boda quebrada.

A delayed wedding, a broken wedding.

3

Cuando lejos de ojo, tan lejos del corazón.

a. When far from sight, far from the heart.
b. Out of sight, out of mind.

4

El amor es el último que resiste morir.

a. Love is the last thing that dies. b. Love dies last.

5

El amor no se exije, se gana.

Love is not demanded, it is earned.

6

El amor obra milagros.

Love works miracles.

1

7

El amor quita el hambre.

a. Love takes away hunger. b. He who is in love seldom thinks of food.

8

El amor vence al odio.

Love conquers hate.

9

El cariño fiel no lo mata la distancia.

True love is not killed by distance.

10

El que ha amado y ha sido amado nació y vivió.

He who has loved and has been loved was born and has lived.

11

En cosas del amor no vale ni las mañas ni la fuerza.

In matters of love, schemes and force are ineffective.

12

En el corazón no se manda.

a. Matters of the heart cannot be commanded.
b. Love occurs naturally.

13

Es más fácil atraer que retener.

It is easier to attract than to retain.

14

Es poquito el amor para perderlo en celos.

Love is too rare to lose it to jealousy.

15

La novia del estudiante no llega ser la esposa del profesionista.

The student's sweetheart does not become the professional's wife.

16

Más vale amar que ser amado.

It is better to love than to be loved.

17

Matrimonio y mortaja del cielo bajan.

a. Marriages and shrouds come down from heaven.
b. Marriages and deaths are decided in heaven.

18

Mucho celo es la destrucción del amor.

a. Much suspicion destroys love. b. Jealousy destroys love.

3

19

No hay nada mejor que amar y ser correspondido.

There is nothing better than to love and be loved in return.

20

No hay que confundir la gratitud con el amor.

One should not mistake gratitude for love.

21

Primero sopitas de miel y después de hiel.

a. First comes honey bread and then bread of bitterness.
b. During courtship there is sweetness and later comes reality.

22

Quien más te quiere te hace llorar.

He who most loves you will make you cry.

23

Quien nunca amó y nunca fue amado jamás nació.

He who never loved and never was loved was never born.

24

Salud, dinero y amor y tiempo para gozarlos.

Health, money and love and time to enjoy them.

25

Vale más quedada, que mal casada.

It is better to be unmarried than to be married to the wrong person.

DICHOS HUMORÍSTICOS/
HUMOROUS SAYINGS

26

A pan duro, diente agudo.

a. Hard bread, sharp-pointed tooth.
b. Hunger makes all bread palatable.

27

A un mentiroso otro mayor.

For every liar there is a greater one.

28

Buen abogado, mal vecino.

A good lawyer, a bad neighbor.

29

Cada chango a su mecate.

a. Each monkey to his rope. b. Each person to his position in life.

30

Cada maestrillo tiene su librillo.

a. Every little master has his little book. b. Every person has a hobby.

31

Cada uno extiende la pierna hasta donde alcanza la cubierta.

Each person stretches his leg as far as the cover will allow.

32

Carne en calceta que la coma quien la meta.

Meat in a stocking should be eaten by the one who puts it there.

33

Casamiento de pobres, fábrica de limosneros.

A wedding between two poor people creates a generation of beggars.

34

Compañía de tres, no vale res.

a. A company of three is not worth a cow's head. b. Three is a crowd.

35

Con el tiempo y un ganchito hasta los de arriba bajan.

a. With time and a little hook, even the ones at the top can be brought down. b. With sufficient time and effort even the mighty can be humbled.

36

Con lo que sana Sancha, Marta cae mala.

From what Sancha recovers, Marta falls ill.

37

De dinero y bondad siempre quita la mitad.

In matters of money and kindness, always take half.

38

Después de un buen taco un buen tabaco.

a. *After a good taco, a good tobacco.*
b. *After a good meal, a good smoke.*

39

El apetito es el mejor cocinero.

a. *Appetite is the best cook.* b. *Hunger is the best motivator.*

40

El ciego no ve pero atienta.

The blind person cannot see but he makes an effort.

41

El hambre es canijo y es más canijo el que lo aguanta.

Hunger is a weakling and more of a weakling is the one who endures it (hunger).

7

42

El hombre propone, Dios dispone, y la mujer descompone.

Man proposes, God disposes, and woman discomposes.

43

El melón y la mujer, malos son de conocer.

The melon and the woman are two things to stay away from.

44

El mozo perezoso por no dar un paso da ocho.

a. The lazy servant to avoid a step will take eight.
b. The lazy person to avoid a task will perform eight.

45

El onceavo, no estorbar.

The eleventh commandment states that you shall not thwart.

46

El prometer no enpobrece.

a. A promise does not impoverish.
b. A promise in itself will not impoverish the promiser.

47

El que con gusto se enreda, que se suelte como pueda.

The person who willingly becomes entangled should free himself any
way he can.

48

El que escupe para arriba, a la cara le cae.

The one who spits upward will find it falls on his face.

49

El que la sigue la consige.

a. He who pursues it will get it.
b. The person who keeps looking for it will find it.

50

El que nace para barrigón, aunque lo fajen de chico.

The person born to be a potbelly will not be helped by being girdled as a child.

51

El que nace para yunque nada más pa' recibir.

The person born to be an anvil will spend his life receiving blows.

52

El que no la corre de joven la corre de viejo.

a. He who does not run around as a young man runs around as an old man.
b. The person who does not sow his oats now will sow them later.

53

El que se fue pa' la villa perdió su silla.

a. He who went to the village lost his chair.
b. He who leaves loses his place.

El que se fue pa' Torreón perdió su sillón.

a. He who went to Torreón City lost his easy chair.
b. He who left lost his place.

55

El que se mete a redendor sale crusíficado.

a. The person who becomes involved in saving ends up crucified.
b. He who tries to be a savior ends up crucified.

56

En casa del herrero, azadón de palo.

At the blacksmith's house, a wooden hoe.

57

En casa del jabonero el que no cae, resbala.

At the soapmaker's home he who does not fall, slips.

58

En casa de tía, pero no cada día.

a. At your aunt's house, but not everyday.
b. Visit your relatives, but not too frequently.

59

En donde hay troncos hay trancazos.

a. Where there are tree trunks there are blows.
b. Where there are weapons there will be conflict.

60

En estas carreteras nomás mis carretas ruedan.

On these highways only my wagons roll.

61

Entre Santa y Santo pared de cal y canto.

To separate a male saint from a female saint, use a stone wall.

62

Están más cerca mis dientes que mis parientes.

My teeth are closer to me than my relatives.

63

Febrero loco y marzo otro poco.

Crazy February and March even more.

64

Goza de tu poco mientras busca más el loco.

Enjoy the little that you have while the fool searches for more.

65

Hacerse el tonto para comer a puños.

Play the fool to accomplish your objectives.

11

66

Hay plumajes que cruzan el pantano y no se manchan.

*There are feathered ones that can cross a pool of stagnant water without
contaminating themselves.*

67

Indio comido, indio ido.

A satisfied Indian is an Indian gone.

68

La lucha es permitida.

It is permissible to attempt the forbidden.

69

La mugre siempre flota.

Filth always floats.

70

La mujer, el vino y el tabaco ponen al hombre flaco.

a. Women, wine and tobacco make a man skinny.
b. Women, wine and tobacco weaken a man.

71

La mujer nació para obedecer y callar.

Woman was born to obey and be silent.

72

La que de amarillo se viste a su belleza se atiene.

She who dresses in yellow must rely on her beauty.

73

Las canas quitan las ganas.

a. Gray hair takes away desire.
b. The years diminish a person's strength.

74

Las canas salen de ganas.

a. Desire causes gray hair. b. Gray hair comes out voluntarily.

75

Las mujeres y el vino hacen errar el camino.

Women and wine cause one to miss the straight road.

76

La suerte de la fea la bonita la desea.

The homely woman's luck is the pretty woman's wish.

77

Lo borracho se quita pero lo feo no.

Drunkenness can be remedied but not ugliness.

78

Lo mismo el chile que aguja, a todos pican igual.

*A hot pepper and a needle have one thing in common; they sting
everyone equally.*

79

Lo que se va a pelar que se vaya remojando.

a. That which is going to be plucked should be soaked first.
b. Before you pluck, make sure you soak.

80

Los parientes y el sol, entre más lejos mejor.

Relatives and the sun, the further away the better.

81

Mejor pan duro que ninguno.

It is better to eat hard bread than none.

82

Muchos cocineros, dañan el puchero.

Too many cooks spoil the stew.

83

Nadie hable mal del día hasta que la noche llegue.

a. No one criticize the day until the night arrives.
b. Do not criticize the day until it is over.

14

84

Nadie sabe lo que tiene el costal, nomás el que lo carga.

No one knows what the sack contains but the person who lugs it.

85

Nadie se va de este mundo vivo.

No one leaves this world alive.

86

No a todos les queda el puro, nomás a los hocicones.

Not everyone was made to smoke a cigar, only those with big lips.

87

No es que sea gorda, lo que pasa es que esta mal fajada.

It is not that she is fat, the problem is that she is badly girdled.

88

No hay loco que coma lumbre.

There is not a madman who is crazy enough to eat fire.

89

No hay mal que por una mujer no venga.

There is no mischief that does not come by way of a woman.

Nadie sabe lo que tiene el costal, nomás el que lo carga.

No me gusta el chisme pero tampoco soy bodega.

a. *I do not like malicious stories but I am not a warehouse.*
b. *I do not approve of gossip but then again I am human.*

Nunca digas de esta agua no beberé.

Never say, "From this water I will never drink."

Palabras de borracho, oídos de mostrador.

a. *Words of a drunkard, hearing the words of one who knows.*
b. *A drunkard will tell you everything that is on his mind.*

Para todo mal, mezcal y para todo bien también.

For every illness drink mezcal (a Mexican liquor) and for good occasions, too.

Parece que no quiebra un plato y tiene el alto roto.

a. *It would seem that she would not break a plate but she has a tall stack of shattered ones.* b. *She is not what she appears to be.*

Quien se hace rico es el que te mantiene el pico.

a. *He who becomes rich is the one who nourishes your beak.*
b. *The one who becomes rich is the one who can provide for your needs.*

96

Si no apesta, no es pata.

If it does not stink, it is not a foot.

97

Si no se hurta se hereda.

If it is not stolen, it is inherited.

98

Si quieres que a tu boda no vaya, envítame por la mañana.

If you do not want me to attend your wedding, invite me the morning before the wedding.

99

Si quieres que yo cante, venga la paga delante.

a. If you want me to sing, let the pay come first.
b. Pay first and the service follows.

100

Si te queda el saco, póntelo.

If the coat fits, put it on.

101

Tanto año de ser condesa y no saber mover el abánico.

a. So many years being a countess and she does not know how to fan herself. b. She has been a countess for many years and she still does not behave like one.

102

Tanto año de ser marinero y no saber nadar.

a. So many years being a seaman to not know how to swim.

b. He has been a sailor so many years and he has not learned to swim.

103

Te tocó carreta, arrástrala.

It was your fortune to have a wagon, now drag it.

104

Trienta años en la marina y no conocer las ranas.

a. Thirty years in the navy and he is not familiar with frogs.

b. He has lived thirty years on the coast and he does not know about frogs.

105

Una cojera de perro y lágrimas de mujer no hay quien las crea.

A dog's limp and a woman's tears are difficult to believe.

106

Unos nacen con estrella y otros nacen estrellados.

a. Some are born under a lucky star and others are born shattered.

b. Some are born advantaged and others are born disadvantaged.

107

Vale más llegar a tiempo que ser envitado.

a. It is better to arrive on time than to be invited.

b. It is better to arrive on time without an invitation than to have an invitation and arrive late.

19

Vale más que haya una loca y no dos.

a. *It is better to have one crazy person and not two.*
b. *The situation is better than we realize.* c. *Things could be worse.*

109

Vale más tuerto que ciego.

It is better to be one-eyed than to be blind.

DICHOS FILOSÓFICOS/
PHILOSOPHICAL SAYINGS

110

A lo hecho, pecho.

a. *To the chest that which is done.* b. *Accept gladly a feat accomplished.*

111

A muertos y a idos no más amigos.

a. *The dead and those that leave are no longer your friends.*
b. *Those that die and those that leave can no longer be relied upon.*

112

Antes de sopa, copa.

a. *Before a piece of bread, a goblet.* b. *Before you eat, a cup of wine.*

113

Arrieros somos y en el camino andamos y un día nos
encontraremos.

a. We are muleteers and on the road we travel and one day we will meet.
b. One day our paths will cross.

114

Cada cabeza es un mundo.

a. Each head is a separate world.
b. Each person has his own way of thinking.

115

Cada cosa se parece a su dueño.

a. Each thing resembles its owner.
b. Each object reflects the owner's personality.

116

Cada quien construye su propio destino.

Each person builds his own destiny.

117

Cuanto más trabajamos más tenemos.

The more we work the more we have.

118

De palo caído todos quieren hacer leña.

From the fallen tree everyone wants firewood.

119

Después de la lluvia sale el sol.

a. After the rain comes the sun. b. After the storm comes the sunshine.

120

De tal amo, tal criado.

a. Like the master, so the servant. b. The master shapes the servant.

121

De tal mata, tal flor.

From such plant, such flower.

122

Donde hay gana, hay maña.

Where there is a will, there is a way.

123

El avaro es capaz de todo lo malo.

The avaricious person is capable of everything evil.

124

El muerto nada se lleva y todo se acaba.

The dead take nothing with them and everything comes to an end.

De tal mata, tal flor.

23

125

El pan ajeno hace el hijo bueno.

a. Strange bread makes a son good.
b. Hard-earned bread makes an offspring strong.

126

El primer paso es el más duro.

a. The first step is the hardest. b. The first move is the most difficult.

127

El orden de los factores no altera el producto.

The order of the factors does not alter the product.

128

El que todo lo quiere todo lo pierde.

a. He who wants it all will lose it all.
b. The greedy person ends up empty-handed.

129

El sabio muda consejo, el necio, no.

The wise man changes his opinion, the foolish man does not.

130

El sombrero y el dinero son los que hacen los amigos.

a. The hat and money will make one friends.
b. Being well-dressed and having money help a person make friends.

131

El trabajo es una mina de oro.

a. Work is a mine of gold. b. From our labor comes riches.

132

El trabajo hace la vida agradable.

Work makes life agreeable.

133

En la unión esta la fuerza.

In union there is strength.

134

Es más rico el rico cuando enpobrece que el pobre cuando enriquese.

The rich person is richer when he becomes poor than the poor person when he becomes rich.

135

Es mejor llorar pobre que llorar solo.

a. It is better to cry poor than to cry alone. b. It is better to be a poor person with friends than a friendless rich person.

136

Favor con favor se paga.

A favor is repaid with a favor.

25

La ciudad es la patria pequeña.

The city is a small fatherland.

La costumbre hace la ley.

Custom forms the law.

La economía es la base de la riqueza.

a. Economy is the foundation of wealth.
b. Prudence is the basis of riches.

La experiencia es madre de ciencia.

a. Experience is the mother of skill. b. One learns from experience.

La limpieza de un lugar es indicio de cultura.

The cleanliness of a place is an indication of culture.

La ocasión hace al ladrón.

The occasion makes the thief.

La ociosidad es madre de todos los vicios.

a. Idleness is the mother of all vices. b. Idleness is the root of all evil.

144

La pobreza es una cosa y la limpieza es otra.

a. Poverty is one thing and cleanliness is another.
b. Poverty is no excuse for not being clean.

145

La salud ante todo.

Health above all else.

146

Las malas noticias vuelven.

a. Bad news returns. b. Bad news comes more than once.

147

La subida más alta tiene la caída más dolorosa.

a. The highest climb has the most painful fall.
b. With the highest climb can come the most painful fall.

148

La verdad siempre sale a flote.

a. The truth always floats. b. The truth eventually surfaces.

149

La vida no retoña.

a. Life does not reappear. b. We have but one life to live.

150

Lo que esta escrito, escrito esta y nadie lo puede cambiar.

That which is written is written and no one can change it.

151

Lo que no se puede remediar, se tiene que aguantar.

What cannot be remedied must be tolerated.

152

Los mejores son los que se van primero.

a. The best are those that go first. b. The best die first.

153

Los ojos son los espejos del alma.

The eyes are the mirrors of the soul.

154

Malo vendrá, que bueno te traerá.

A bad occurrence can bring you something pleasant.

155

Marzo ventoso y abril lluvioso, hace a mayo hermoso.

The winds of March and the showers of April bring the beauty of May.

156

Más vale la alegría en la pobreza, que inquietudes en la riqueza.

Happiness in poverty is superior to wealth with anxiety.

157

Más vale saber que haber.

It is better to know than to have.

158

Mi casa es su casa.

My house is your house.

159

Mientras en casa estoy, rey soy.

While in my home, I am king.

160

Mientras hay vida hay esperanza.

While there is life there is hope.

161

Mucho va de Pedro a Pedro.

a. There is a wide difference between Peter and Peter.
b. Humans vary greatly in personality and talent.

29

Mi casa es su casa.

162

Nadie es profeta en su tierra.

No one is a prophet in his own land.

163

Ni un dedo hace mano ni una golondrina verano.

One finger does not a hand make nor does one swallow springtime make.

164

No hay presente sin futuro.

a. There is not a present without a future. b. Each today has a tomorrow. c. What one does today affects the future.

165

Obra de común, obra de ningún.

a. A work which belongs to the community belongs to no one person.
b. A project completed by many cannot be claimed by one individual.

166

Pereza es la madre de la pobreza.

Laziness is the mother of poverty.

167

Poquito veneno no mata.

a. A little poison will not kill.
b. A small amount of poison will not kill you.

168

Quien nada hace nada vale.

He who does (makes) nothing is worth nothing.

169

Todo es del color del cristal tras que se mira.

a. *Everything is the color of the crystal from which it is seen.*
b. *Everything is a reflection of the mirror from which it is seen.*

170

Tras los años viene el juicio.

With the years comes wisdom.

171

Uno da la idea y pone a un ejército a trabajar.

One provides the idea and then puts an army to work.

172

Un padre para cien hijos, y no cien hijos para un padre.

*One parent can support one hundred children but one hundred children
will not support one parent.*

173

Vale más gotera que dure y no chorro que se acabe.

A trickle that lasts is worth more than a stream that soon ends.

174

Vida sin amigos, muerte sin testigos.

a. A life without friends, a death without witnesses.
b. A friendless life, a forlorn death.

DICHOS RELIGIOSOS/RELIGIOUS SAYINGS

175

A cada capillita se le llega su función.

a. Each little chapel has its day of celebration.
b. Each person will have his day of reward.

176

A cada santo se le llega su hora de celebración.

a. Each saint has his day of celebration.
b. Each person's day will come.

177

Achaques quiere el diablo.

a. The devil wants pretexts. b. The devil thrives on excuses.

178

Amá a tu vecino y te amará.

a. Love your neighbor and he will love you.
b. Respect your neighbor and he will respect you.

33

179

A quien Dios quiere bien, uvas le da el laurel.

a. *The laurel will give grapes to the one whom God loves.*
b. *Prosperity will come to the one whom God blesses.*

180

Cada quien siente lo suyo y Dios siente lo de todos.

Everyone feels for his own and God feels for everyone.

181

Cada uno en su casa y Dios en la de todos.

Everyone in his home and God in everyone's.

182

Cuando Dios no quiere, angeles no pueden.

The angels cannot grant that which God will not permit.

183

Da a Dios lo que es de Dios, y a Cesar lo que es de Cesar.

a. *Give to God what is God's and to Caesar what is Caesar's.*
b. *Give to each what is his.*

184

De los arrepentidos se sirve Dios.

a. *God serves himself from those who repent.*
b. *God is pleased with those who repent.*

185

De puerta cerrada el diablo se vuelve.

From a closed door the devil goes away.

186

Dios castiga el escándalo más que el crimen.

God punishes the scandal (exposure) more than the crime.

187

Dios es más grande que tus problemas.

a. God is bigger than your problems.
b. God can solve your biggest problems.

188

Dios le da alas a las hormigas para morir más pronto.

a. God provides wings to ants so that they will die more quickly.
b. Sometimes a blessing can become a curse.

189

Dios le da habas a quien no tiene quijadas.

a. God provides beans to the person who has no jaw.
b. God sometimes provides to the person who no longer can enjoy.

190

Dios los cría y ellos se juntan.

a. God creates them and they unite.
b. Similar individuals come together.

191

Dios no le dió alas a los alacranes.

God did not give wings to scorpions.

192

Dios sabe lo que hace.

God has a reason for what He does.

193

El camino al infierno esta cubierto de rosas.

The road to hell is covered with roses.

194

El rosario alrededor del cuello, y el diablo en el cuerpo.

The rosary around one's neck and the devil in one's body.

195

Es más facil que entre un elefante por el ojo de una aguja que un rico a la gloria.

It is easier for an elephant to pass through the eye of a needle than for a rich person to enter paradise.

196

La cruz en el pecho y el diablo en los hechos.

a. The cross on one's chest and the devil in one's actions.
b. He has a cross on his chest and the devil in his deeds.

197

Más vale vergüenza en la cara que mancha en el corazón.

a. Shame on one's face is superior to a stain on one's heart.
b. It is better to confess one's sins than to conceal one's guilt.

198

No hay virtud más alta que el perdón.

There is no higher virtue than forgiveness.

199

O todos hijos de Dios, o todos hijos del diablo.

a. Either all are children of God or all are children of the devil.
b. All persons should be treated equally.

200

Sin encomendarse a Dios ni al diablo.

a. To entrust oneself neither to God nor to the devil. b. He embarked on his foolish scheme without consulting with God or the devil.

201

Venganza es placer de Dios.

Vengeance belongs to God.

DICHOS CONSEJEROS/
SAYINGS THAT ADVISE

202

A donde vayas, haz lo que veas.

a. Wherever you go, do as you see.
b. When in Rome, do as the Romans do.

203

A la mala costumbre, quiébrale la pata.

a. Break a bad habit's leg. *b. It is wise to eliminate one's bad habits.*

204

A la mejor persona se le van las patas.

a. The best person can lose his feet.
b. A person of high morals can commit a transgression.

205

Al buen entendedor basta con pocas palabras.

One who really understands needs few words of explanation.

206

A menos palabras menos plietos.

a. Fewer words, fewer disputes. *b. The fewer words the better.*

207

Año nuevo, vida nueva.

a. New year, new life. *b. A new year brings new opportunities.*

208

Arrímate a los buenos y serás uno de ellos.

Get close to good people and you will be one of them.

209

A veces querer no es poder.

a. Sometimes to want is not enough.
b. Sometimes those who want do not have the power to obtain.

210

Buen principio, la mitad es hecha.

With a good beginning, half the task is done.

211

Cada quien su vida.

a. Each one to his own life. b. Live and let live.

212

Cuando llueve y hace viento, cierra la puerta y quédate adentro.

a. When it rains and it is windy, close the door and stay inside.
b. When there is trouble brewing outside, stay inside.

213

Cuando te compran, vende, y cuando te venden, compra.

When they want to buy from you, sell, and when they want to sell to you, buy.

214

Cuéntale tus penas a quien te las pueda remediar.

Tell your sorrows to someone who can help you.

215

Cuida tu casa y deja la ajena.

a. Take care of your home and forsake another's. b. Look after your own home and do not be concerned with your neighbor's.

216

De la calle vendrán y de tu casa te echarán.

a. From the street they will come and from your home they will eject you. b. One never knows who will force one to leave one's home.

217

De lo perdido, lo que aparesca.

a. Of what is lost, whatever comes up. b. Of what is lost, whatever you can recover. c. Something is better than nothing.

218

De lo que te sobra repartes.
a. Of what remains, distribute. b. Divide among your loved ones that which you do not need.

219

Después del daño, cada uno es sabio.

After the accident, everyone is a sage.

220

Donde lumbre hubo, rescoldos quedan.

a. *Where there was a fire, embers remain.*
b. *Where an incident occurred, signs remain.*

221

Donde una puerta se cierra, otra se abre.

a. *Where one door is closed, another one is opened.*
b. *When one opportunity fades, another one appears.*

222

El agua y el aceite nunca se juntan.

a. *Water and oil never mix.* b. *Some things in this world never unite.*

223

El campo fértil no descansado, se tornará estéril.

The fertile field which is not given rest will become barren.

224

El ejercicio hace al maestro.

Labor produces the master.

225

El mejor consejo es la experiencia pero llega tarde.

The best advice is experience but experience comes late in life.

226

El negocio es uno y el parentesco es otro.

Business is one thing and kinship is another.

227

El que da primero da dos veces.

The one who gives first gives twice.

228

El que da razón del camino es que andado lo tiene.

The one who can tell you what to expect along the road is the one who has traveled that road.

229

El que hoy cae, mañana se levanta.

a. He who falls today will rise tomorrow.
b. The person who is down today will be up tomorrow.

230

El que mucho habla, poco logra.

He who talks much accomplishes little.

231

El que nada debe nada teme.

a. He who does not owe does not fear.
b. The person who has no debts has nothing to dread.

232

El que nada, no se ahoga.

a. He who swims will not drown.
b. He who perseveres will not perish.

233

El que no ariezga, no pasa el charco.

He who does not take a risk does not cross the puddle.

234

El que no se avienta no crusa la mar.

He who does not move does not cross the sea.

235

El tiempo perdido no se recupera jamás.

Wasted time can never be recovered.

236

En la necesida se conocen los amigos.

In times of need, you learn who your friends are.

237

En la tardanza esta el peligro.

In tardiness there is risk.

238

En padres y hermanos no metan las manos.

In matters between parents and children, do not interfere.

239

Entre más abarcas menos avanzas.

a. *The more you undertake, the less you can accomplish.*
b. *Too many things undertaken at once, little accomplished.*

240

Es de sabios cambiar de opinión.

a. *Wise men can change their opinion.*
b. *To change a judgment is the province of wise men.*

241

Es mejor mancha en la frente que manchita en el corazón.

It is better to have a spot on one's forehead than a stain on one's heart.

242

Hasta la paciencia de los santos tiene limite.

Even the patience of saints has a limit.

243

Hay que recordar que hay unos más grandes que uno.

We must recognize that there are some who are greater than we are.

244

Hay que respectar las canas.

a. One should respect gray hair. b. We should respect our elders.

245

Hay que sufrir para merecer.

One must suffer to be worthy.

246

Hay unos que deben muertes y ni la cárcel pisan.

a. There are those who owe for deaths and have not stepped inside a jail.
b. The guilty are not always punished.

247

Hijo no tener y nombre le poner.

a. Not having a son and giving him a name. b. Do not name your sons until they are born. c. Do not count your chickens before they hatch.

248

La caridad empieza por tu casa.

Charity begins at home.

249

La educación es la única cosa que nadie te podrá quitar.

Education is the only thing which no one can take away from you.

250

La envidia es mala consejera.

Envy is a bad adviser.

251

La letra con sangre entra.

a. Learning with blood enters. b. Learning requires sacrifice.

252

La mentira es la destrucción de la felicidad.

a. Mendacity can destroy happiness. b. A lie can destroy blissfulness.

253

La mujer nació para cargar la cruz.

Woman was born to carry the cross.

254

La mujer se hizo para la casa y el hombre para el trabajo.

Woman was made for the household and man for hard labor.

255

La ropa hace al hombre.

Garments make the man.

256

Las desgracias no llegan solas.

a. Misfortunes do not come alone. b. Adversities do not come singly.

257

Las palabras vuelan, los escritos quedan.

Speech flies but writing endures.

258

Las palabras y las promesas se las lleva el viento.

Words and promises are blown away by the wind.

259

La tercera es la vencida.

a. The third one is the one you will subdue.
b. The third time is when you will succeed.

260

Lo barato cuesta caro.

a. That which is cheap is costly. b. Cheap things do not last.

261

Lo más claro es lo más decente.

a. The clearer the better. b. The decent thing to do is to tell the truth.

262

Lo que no fue en tu año, no fue en tu daño.

a. What did not occur during your time was not done to harm you.
b. Do not worry about a happening that occurred before you and I met.

263

Lo que uno no puede ver, en su casa lo ha de tener.

a. What one cannot tolerate, one can find in one's home.
b. Those things that one abhors can be found in one's home.

264

Los mejores amigos son los buenos libros.

a. The best friends are good books. b. Your best friend is knowledge.

265

Los que nacen en diciembre nacen con buena estrella.

Those born in December are born under a good star.

266

Más vale que sobre que no que falte.

It is better to have too much than not enough.

267

Mejor vecino cerca que hermano lejos.

It is better to have a neighbor nearby than a brother far away.

268

No firmes cartas que no leas ni bebas agua que no veas.

*Do not sign letters that you have not read nor drink water that you have
    not examined.*

269

No hay tiempo como el presente.

a. There is no time like the present.
b. The best time to undertake a task is now.

270

No mojes tu pluma en el tintero del patrón.

a. Do not dip your fountain pen in the boss's inkwell.
b. Do not avail yourself of your employer's property.

271

No te burles del vecino, y no ofendas al amigo.

Do not make fun of your neighbor and do not offend a friend.

272

No todo el que chifla es arriero.

a. Not everyone who whistles is a muleteer.
b. Do not be fooled by appearances.

273

No se tomó Zamora en una hora.

a. Zamora City was not taken in one hour.
b. It takes time to accomplish big deeds.

274

Nunca dejes camino por vereda.

Never leave a road for a path.

275

Nunca pretendas ser lo que jamás podrás ser.

Never pretend to be that which you will never be.

276

Palo blanco abarca todo campo.

a. The white tree occupies all the field.
b. A common tree occupies valuable space.

277

Para muestra, con un botón basta.

a. For a sample, a button is enough.
b. If you want a sample of the merchandise, a portion suffices.

278

Para que es tanto brinco estando el cielo tan parejo.

a. Why is there so much jumping when the sky is so even?
b. Why try so hard when the goal is easy to reach?

279

¿Para que llorar sobre leche desparramada?

Why cry over spilled milk?

280

¿Para que quieres un pedazo de pastel si lo puedes tener todo?

Why be satisfied with a piece of cake if you can have it all?

Piedra que rueda nunca hace moho.

A rolling stone never gathers moss.

282

Poco a poco hila la vieja el copo.

a. Little by little the old woman spins the bundle of cotton.
b. Little by little the task can be accomplished.

283

Preguntando se llega a Roma.

a. He who asks will arrive in Rome. b. Ask and you will find a way.

284

Pronto pasará la tormenta y volverá la luz del sol.

Soon will pass the storm and the sun's light will return.

285

Quien adelante no mira, atrás se queda.

a. The person who cannot see ahead will stay behind.
b. He who cannot look ahead will not progress.

286

Quien busca, halla.

a. He who searches, finds. b. He who seeks will find a way.

287

Quien evita la ocasión evita el peligrón.

The person who avoids the occasion avoids the danger.

288

Quien hizo la ley también hizo la trampa.

The person who made the law also made the snare.

289

Quien no se aventura no pasa la mar.

He who does not take a chance does not cross the sea.

290

Quien persiste en su maldad seguirá tejiendo su desdichado destino.

The one who persists in his wickedness will continue weaving his miserable destiny.

291

Quien se viste de mal paño, dos veces se viste al año.

a. The person who dresses in poor cloth dresses twice a year.
b. The person who is a poor dresser seldom is invited (to social functions).

292

Quien temprano se levanta tiene una hora más de vida y en su trabajo adelanta.

The early riser has an additional hour of life and progresses in his work.

293

Quien tiene tejado de vidrio, no tire piedras al de su vecino.

He who has a glass house should not throw stones at his neighbor's house.

294

Quien va despacio y con tiento hace dos cosas a tiempo.

He who proceeds slowing and with prudence does two things at the same time.

295

Roma no se hizo en un día.

a. *Rome was not built in a day.*
b. *It takes a long time to accomplish something worthwhile.*

296

Si no haces el juego, no hagas las reglas.

If you are not in the game, do not make the rules.

297

Si quieres buena fama, que no te dé el sol en la cama.

If you want a good reputation, do not let the sun (day) find you in bed.

298

Si quieres ser bien servido, sírvete a ti mismo.

If you want to be well served, serve yourself.

299

Si quieres vivir en paz, lo que sabes no dirás y lo que ves no
    juzgarás.

*If you want to live in peace, what you know you will not tell and what
    you see you will not judge.*

300

Si rasuran al vecino pon tu barba a remojar.

a. If your neighbor is being shaved, begin soaking your beard.
b. What happens to your neighbor may happen to you.

301

Si tiras la piedra no escondas la mano.

If you throw the rock do not hide your hand.

302

Si tu mal tiene remedio para que te apuras, y si no lo tiene,
    para que te apuras.

If your illness has a remedy why worry, and if it does not, why worry.

303

Solitos bajan al agua sin que nadie los arree.

*a. They will go to the water without being driven. b. It is not
    necessary to force an animal to drink water. c. There is no need to
    force people to do those things which they will do naturally.*

304

Tiempo tras tiempo viene.

Better times are sure to come.

305

Una buena acción vale tanto como una obra maestra.

a. A good act is worth as much as a masterpiece.
b. A good deed is equivalent to a masterpiece.

306

Vale más rodear que no rodar.

It is better to go around than to not move at all.

307

Vete por la sombra porque por el sol te quemas.

Take the shady path because the sun will burn you.

308

Viejo el aire y todavía sopla.

Old is the wind and it still blows.

309

Viejo el mar y todavía se mueve.

Old is the sea and it still moves.

310

Viejo el sol y todavía brilla.

a. Old is the sun and it still shines.
b. An old thing can still be serviceable.

311

Viejo los cerros y todavía dan flores.

Old are the hills and they still have flowers.

Viejo los cerros y todiavía dan flores.

57

DICHOS PSICOLÓGICOS/
PSYCHOLOGICAL SAYINGS

312

Acompáñate con los buenos y serás uno de ellos.

a. Go with the good and you will be one of them.
b. Associate with decent people and you will be one of them.

313

Aguántate tantito y la fruta caidrá en tu mano.

a. Wait a little while and the fruit will fall into your hand.
b. Be patient and things will go your way.

314

A mal tiempo buena cara.

During times of misfortune, present a cheerful face.

315

A veces la música ablanda el corazón de las fieras.

Sometimes harmony can soften a cruel heart.

316

Bajo su capa de manso cordero se oculta un cruel león.

Underneath the coat of a gentle lamb hides a cruel lion.

Cada persona es un mundo.

Each person is a separate reality.

Cada quien siente su mal.

Each person must suffer his own grief.

Con los años vienen los desengaños.

With the years come disappointments.

Con paciencia y un ganchito, hasta una fortuna se alcanza.

With patience and a little hook, even a fortune can be obtained.

Cortesía de boca, mucho vale y poco cuesta.

Courteous words are very valuable and cost little.

Cuando se ha vivido mal se aprende a desconfiar de todos.

When one has lived immorally, one learns to distrust everyone.

Cuando suben los honores, suben los dolores.

a. As the honors mount, the pain mounts.
b. As a person's status increases, his problems increase.

324

De la desconfianza nace la seguridad.

a. From distrust is born security. b. From mistrust comes safety.

325

Dicen que también de dolor se canta cuando llorar no se
    puede.

It is said that anguish is revealed through singing when one cannot cry.

326

Conde fuego hubo, cenizas quedan.

a. Where a conflagration occurred, ashes remain.
b. Where an occurrence took place, evidence remains.

327

Dos amigos de una bolsa, uno canta y otro llora.

a. Two friends from one money bag, one sings and the other cries.
b. When two friends enter into a business venture, one prospers and the
    other suffers.

328

El bondadoso y el noble saben ser felices y hacen felices a los
  demás.

*The kind person and the noble person are familiar with happiness and
  make others happy as well.*

329

El flojo trabaja doble.

a. The lazy person works twice as hard.
*b. The lazy individual works twice as hard in his efforts to avoid
  work.*

330

El interés tiene pies.

a. Self-interest has feet. b. Selfishness is a great mover.

331

El miedoso de su sombra huye.

The fearful person flees from his shadow.

332

El pan comido, la compañía deshecha.

a. The bread eaten, the guests leave.
b. The guests leave when there is no more to eat.
c. Your friends leave you when you have no more to give.

El primer pensamiento es el mejor.

Your first idea is the best one.

334

El que es centavo aunque ande revuelto entre los pesos.

The person who is a penny will remain a penny even though he associates with dollars.

335

El que hace más de lo que puede, hace más de lo que debe.

The one who does more than he is able, does more than his duty (share).

336

El que mantiene, detiene, si no ni derecho tiene.

a. The one who sustains you constrains you, otherwise he would have no right.
b. If a person supports you, he has a right to restrict you.

337

El que mata una vez no le importa hacerlo de nuevo.

The one who kills once does not mind doing it again.

338

El que tiempo agarra tiempo le sobra.

He who uses his time wisely has time to spare.

El que va despacio llega lejos.

He who is cautious goes far.

El tiempo cura toda herida.

Time heals all wounds.

El tiempo todo lo cura o todo lo borra.

Time either heals everything or erases it.

El trabajo revive al hombre.

a. Work revives the man. b. Work motivates the human spirit.

En buen día, buenas obras.

a. On a good day, good works.
b. Good work can be produced on a good day.

En el querer esta el poder.

a. In the will is the ability.
b. In the will lies the ability to accomplish.

Enemigo que huye, puente de plata.

Provide a silver bridge for a fleeing enemy.

En la cara esta la edad.

One's age is reflected on one's face.

Entre dos amigos un notario y dos testigos.

a. Between two friends, use a notary public and two witnesses.
b. Even among friends, legal precautions should be taken.

Farol de la calle y oscuridad de su casa.

a. A street lantern and darkness in the home.
b. They show one face in public and another at home.

Hay que regresar la copa.

a. One should return the goblet. b. One always should return a favor.

Hombre prevenido nunca fué vencido.

A careful person never was (is) defeated.

351

Inocente para siempre se lo lleva la corriente.

The one who remains simple-minded will be swept away by the current.

352

La caridad por uno empieza.

Charity begins with oneself.

353

La confianza mata al hombre.

a. Unfounded trust kills the man. b. Groundless trust can be costly.

354

La confianza mata la amistad.

a. Familiarity kills a friendship. b. Familiarity breeds contempt.

355

La confianza no se da, se gana.

Trust is not given, it is earned.

356

Las amistades se conocen al estar enfermo o en la cárcel.

You know who your friends are when you are ill or incarcerated.

357

Las apariencias engañan.

Appearances can deceive.

358

Las cosas hablando se entienden.

Things become clear through communication.

359

La virtud y la honestidad se pierden muy fácil.

Honesty and chastity are lost very easily.

360

Lo que con los padres hagan con los hijos lo pagan.

a. What a person does to his parents will be repaid to him by his children.
b. As you treat your parents, so will your children treat you.

361

Lo que en el capillo se toma con la martaja se deja.

a. That which is grasped with a child's cap is laid away with the shroud.
b. What is learned as a child remains with a person throughout life.

362

Lo que no ven no quieren.

What one does not see, one does not want.

363

Los pecados que pesan en la conciencia no suelen reflejarse en el rostro.

The sins that bother your conscience will not show on your face.

364

Más fatigan los placeres que los negocios.

a. Pleasure is more tiring than work.
b. The pursuit of pleasure is more fatiguing than toil.

365

Más hace el que quiere, que el que puede y no quiere.

More is accomplished by the one who wants to than by the one who can and does not want to.

366

Más puede maña que fuerza.

Cleverness is stronger than force.

367

Más sabe el tonto en su casa que el sabio en la ajena.

a. The fool knows more in his home than does a wise man in another's home. b. An ignorant person knows more about his bailiwick than does a sage.

368

Más tiene el rico de pobre que el pobre de rico.

a. The rich person has more of the poor than the poor person has of the rich. b. The rich person has more characteristics of a poor person than the poor person has characteristics of a rich person.

369

Más vale no ponerse en el tocadero.

It is better to not put yourself where danger lurks.

370

Mente sana, cuerpo sano.

Sound mind, sound body.

371

Nada hay peor que prometer y fallar.

There is nothing worse than to promise and then to fail to fulfill your promise.

372

Nadie sea tuerto y nadie se lo dirá.

a. Do not be one-eyed and no one will mention it to you.
b. Eliminate your defects and you will be free of criticism.

373

No es madre la que tiene a los hijos sino quien los cría.

The one who bears children is not the mother but the one who rears them.

374

No hagas promesas que no puedes cumplir.

Do not make promises that you cannot fulfill.

375

No hay mejor espejo que el amigo viejo.

a. There is no better mirror than an old friend.
b. The best reflection of oneself is an old friend.

376

No hay peor sordo que el que no quiere oír.

a. The worst deaf man is the one who does not want to hear.
b. There is nothing as sad as the person who does not want to hear the truth.

377

No hay rosa sin espinas.

a. There is not a rose without thorns.
b. Every life has its share of pain.

378

No hay tiempo malo si el trabajo es bueno.

a. There are no bad times if the work is good.
b. Time flies when you enjoy your work.

279

No puedes andar y quieres correr.

a. You cannot walk and still you want to run. b. First things first.

380

O todos hijos o todos entenados.

a. Either all are children or all are stepchildren.
b. Everyone should be treated equally.

No hay rosa sin espinas.

Paciencia es inteligencia.

Patience is intelligence.

Pagan justos por pecadores.

a. The just pay for the sinners. b. The innocent pay for the guilty.

Quien adelante no mira, atrás se queda.

The person who does not look ahead stays behind.

Quien no se da a respetar merece que nadie lo respete.

a. The person who does not respect himself deserves that no one should respect him.
b. You will not be respected unless you respect yourself.

Quien tiene arte va a todas partes.

The person with talent has no limits.

Sé indulgente con otros y lo serán contigo.

Be kind to others and they will be kind to you.

387

Se sufre pero se aprende.

a. One suffers but one learns. b. One learns from suffering.

388

Si uno no quiere, dos no pelean.

a. If one is not willing, two will not fight.
b. It takes two to make a quarrel.

389

Sobre advertencia no hay engaño.

a. On being warned there is no deceit.
b. There is no misunderstanding once you have been counseled.

390

Sobre gusto no hay dispuestas.

a. Over taste there is no basis. b. One cannot account for a person's fancy. c. There is no accounting for taste.

391

Tal padre, tal hijo.

a. Like father, like son. b. The father forms the son.

392

Una cosa es la instrucción y otra es la educación.

Education is one thing and breeding (social behavior) is another.

393

Un fracaso no quiere decir que la batalla esta perdida.

One misfortune does not mean that the battle is lost.

394

Un hombre sin alegría no esta bueno o no es bueno.

a. A sad man either is not in good health or is not a good person.
b. An unhappy person is either in bad health or is a bad person.

395

Uno nunca debe confiarse en las apariencias.

One should not rely on appearances.

396

Unos nacieron para mandar y otros para obedecer.

Some were born to give orders and others to obey.

DICHOS DE ANIMALES/
SAYINGS ABOUT ANIMALS

397

Al buen caballo no lo canse.

a. Do not exhaust a good horse.
b. Do not ruin the horse that wins the races.

398

Al caballo regalado no se le miran los dientes.

Do not look a gift horse in the mouth.

399

Asno de muchos, lobos le comen.

a. An untended donkey will be eaten by the wolves.
b. Everyone's business is no one's business.

400

Ave de mucha pluma poca carne.

a. A bird of many feathers, little flesh.
b. Much appearance but little substance.

401

Cada asno con su tamaño.

a. Each donkey with his size. b. Each donkey seeks out a donkey.
c. Like seeks like.

402

Cuando el burro te tumba hasta los perros te muerden.

When a donkey knocks you down, even the dogs bite you.

403

Cuando el perro aulle, el hombre muere.

When the dog howls, the man dies.

404

Cuando el tecolote canta, el indio muere.

When the owl hoots, the Indian dies.

405

El buey lerdo bebe agua turbia.

a. The slow ox will drink muddy water.
b. The dull person will commit addle-brained acts.

406

El buey viejo bien se lame.

a. The old ox licks himself well. b. Practice makes perfect.

407

El hijo de la rata ratones mata.

a. The son of the rat kills mice. b. Like father, like son.

408

El lavarle el hocico al puerco es perder jabón y tiempo.

To wash a hog's snout is a waste of soap and time.

409

El mayor de los males es tratar con animales.

The worst of imperfections is to have conversations with animals.

El perro que vive con hambre va a tragar dondequiera.

a. The dog that lives with hunger will eat anywhere.
b. A hungry dog is not particular where he eats.

El que toma la zorra y la desuella, ha de saber más que ella.

a. He who catches a fox and skins it is more clever than the fox.
b. A clever person sometimes finds his equal.

Gato con guantes no caza ratón.

a. A cat that wears gloves will not chase a mouse.
b. A man in a suit will not do hard labor.

Hijo de tigre, tigrillo.

a. Son of a tiger, baby tiger. b. Wild father, wild son.

La mula es mula; cuando no patea, vuela.

a. A mule is a mule; when it does not kick, it moves swiftly.
b. There are times when you can get a mule to do what you want.

La zorra mudará los dientes mas no las mientes.

A fox may lose its teeth but not its nature.

416

Nadie quiere comprar un caballo dormido.

No one wants to buy a sleeping horse.

417

No hace tanto la zorra en un año como paga en una hora.

a. The fox does not do in one year what it pays in one hour.
b. Craftiness may temporarily succeed but the day of reckoning is a
   certainty.

418

No le busques tres picos al toro.

a. Do not look for three horns on the bull.
b. Do not make a problem more complicated than it is.

419

No se hizo la miel para la boca del asno.

a. Honey was not made for the donkey's mouth.
b. We should not waste good things on the undeserving.

420

Para cada perro hay su garrote.

a. For each dog there is an appropriate stick.
b. For each problem there is a solution.

421

Para matar a la chinche hay que quemar el petate.

To kill the bedbug, one must burn the sleeping mat.

Perro ladrador, poco mordedor.

a. A barking dog little bites. b. Seldom does a barking dog bite.

Perro que lame no engorda.

A dog that licks will not grow fat.

Por la boca muere el pez.

a. Through the mouth dies the fish.
b. The mouth can be one's downfall.

Quien quiere a Romero quiere a su perro.

a. He who likes Romero likes his dog.
b. He who likes a man should also like his dog.

Si se muere el perro, se acaba la rabia.

a. If the dog dies, the rabies will cease.
b. Eliminate the source of the problem and the problem will disappear.

Todas las aves con sus pares.

a. All birds with their kind. b. Birds of a feather flock together.